DRAWING
Fascinating Animals

BY ABBY COLICH

ILLUSTRATED BY COLIN HOWARD

raintree
a Capstone company — publishers for children

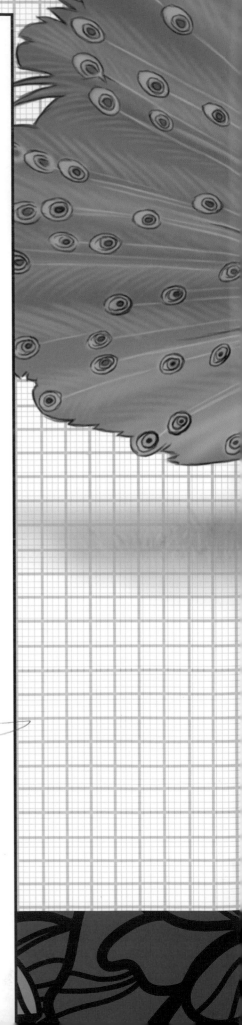

Raintree is an imprint of Capstone Global Library Limited, a company incorporated in England and Wales having its registered office at 7 Pilgrim Street, London, EC4V 6LB – Registered company number: 6695582

www.raintree.co.uk
myorders@raintree.co.uk

Edited by Abby Colich

Designed by Juliette Peters and Charmaine Whitman

Cover designed by Aruna Rangarajan

Illustrated by Juan Calle

Production by Laura Manthe

ISBN 978 1 4062 9434 7
18 17 16 15 14
10 9 8 7 6 5 4 3 2 1

British Library Cataloguing in Publication Data
A full catalogue record for this book is available from the British Library.

Printed and bound in China.

Contents

Getting started

From beautiful blue butterflies to the fabulously feathered peacock, the world is full of fascinating animals. Animals are fun to learn about and fun to draw, too. Whether you're skilled at sketching or new to the world of drawing, you can have fun filling pages with a wide variety of animals.

Peacock

The peacock is known for its dramatic tail feather display. These bright feathers are covered in shades of green, blue, and gold. A dark blue marking on each feather in the shape of an eye is surrounded by other vibrant shades.

Step 1

Step 2

Step 3

Step 4

Final

TIP

The peacock doesn't always walk around with its feathers upright. Draw the peacock with its feathers down behind its back.

22

23

Each activity includes a description of the animal, steps to show you exactly how to draw each creature, and a tip for when you want to get creative and try something new. If your hummingbird looks horrible or your flamingo is flawed, don't worry. Drawing takes practice. If you make a mistake, it's OK to start again. Just remember to be creative and have fun while you work.

4

Tools of the trade

Drawing is a fun and inexpensive way to express yourself and your creativity. Before you get started, make sure you have the proper tools.

Paper

Any white paper will work, but a sketchbook specifically for drawing is best.

Pencils

Any pencil will do, but many artists prefer graphite pencils made especially for drawing.

Colour

A good set of coloured pencils will give you many options for colour. You can also try using felt-tip pens or paint. Many artists enjoy outlining and filling in their work with artist pens.

Sharpener

Your pencils will be getting a lot of use, so make sure you have a sturdy sharpener. A good sharpener will give your pencil a nice, sharp point.

Rubber

Be sure to get a good rubber. Choose a rubber that won't leave smudges on your clean, white paper.

Drawing on screen

Many great apps and computer programs allow you to draw on screen rather than on paper. If you want to give this medium a try, ask an adult to help you get started. Learn all the features and functions before you begin.

Blue Morpho butterfly

This beautiful insect shows off four bright blue wings edged with black. Scales on the wings reflect light, giving them their blue hue. This butterfly is one of the world's largest with a wingspan of 13 to 20 centimetres.

Step 1

Step 2

TIP

Draw the morpho with its wings closed. The backs of its wings are a dull brown with eyespots that help to camouflage it from predators.

Step 3

Step 4

Final

Blue Dasher dragonfly

These beautiful insects are not your typical creepy crawlies. Dragonflies have four large transparent wings and slender bodies. The male dashers are blue. The females are usually black and yellow.

Step 1

Step 2

TIP

There are plenty of other dragonfly species to draw. Perhaps the red-veined darter will inspire you. Can you guess what colour it is?

Step 3

Step 4

Final

Ruby-Throated hummingbird

These hummingbirds have metallic green and white feathers, but only the males have a bright red throat. Hummingbirds flap their wings so quickly that they make a humming noise. Their short and stubby legs prevent them from walking or standing, so they are always on the move.

Step 1

Step 2

TIP

Hummingbirds are like acrobats. Can you draw one flying upside down?

Step 3

Step 4

Final

Snowy owl

Snowy owls are born with spots that lighten as they age. Males eventually turn mostly white, while females keep some spots on their wings. Their white feathers help them to blend in with their Arctic surroundings. Don't forget the sharp talons when sketching this bird. The owl uses these claws to catch its prey.

Step 1

Step 2

TIP

Each wing of the snowy owl is longer than the length of its body. Draw this majestic bird flying with its wings spread.

Step 3

Step 4

Final

Huacaya alpaca

Huacaya alpacas are one of two alpaca breeds. Alpacas are fluffy creatures that resemble llamas. They are raised in South America for their fur. The soft fur is used to make blankets and clothing. Alpaca fur can be many different shades of white, brown and black.

TIP

The Suri is the other breed of alpaca. You can draw a Suri by giving your alpaca longer, shaggier hair.

Step 3

Step 4

Final

Flamingo

This pink bird spends its days wading in warm waters, usually standing on one leg with the other tucked beneath its body. It sticks its long, curved neck down into the water and grabs crustaceans with its black-tipped bill. The flamingo's diet of crustaceans is what makes its feathers pink.

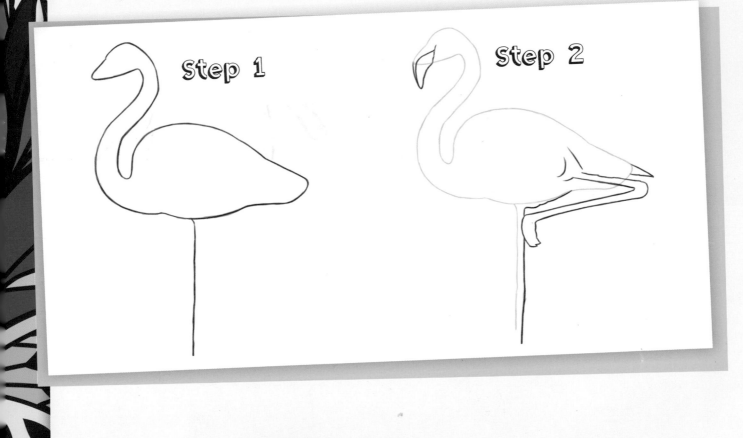

TIP

You can draw this bird in flight with its wings extended out and its body stretched long. The undersides of its wings are black.

Step 3

Step 4

Final

Gentoo penguin

A white-feathered cap is one of the identifying features of the Gentoo penguin. This creature also has a bright orange-red beak and peach-coloured feet. These penguins are the fastest swimmers of all diving birds, moving up to 35 kilometres per hour.

Step 1

Step 2

TIP

A Gentoo penguin makes as many as 450 dives each day for food. Can you draw this bird diving into icy waters in search of food?

Step 3

Step 4

Final

Frilled lizard

This lizard has an unusual feature – a frill of leathery, scaly skin around its head. When feeling threatened, the lizard opens its frill and hisses while standing on its hind legs. Then it runs on its hind legs until it finds a tree, and climbs to safety.

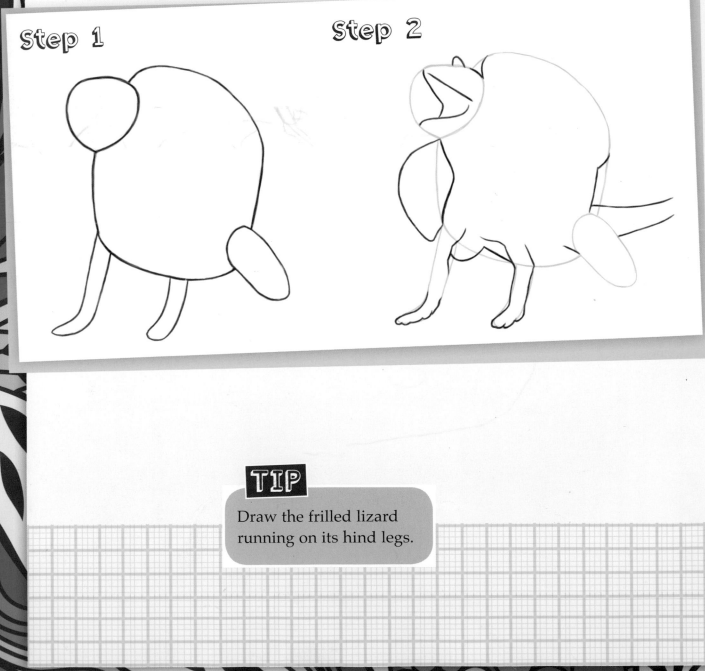

Step 1

Step 2

TIP

Draw the frilled lizard running on its hind legs.

Step 3

Step 4

Final

21

Peacock

The peacock is known for its dramatic tail feather display. These bright feathers are covered in shades of green, blue and gold. A dark blue marking on each feather in the shape of an eye is surrounded by other vibrant shades.

Step 1

Step 2

 TIP

The peacock doesn't always walk around with its feathers upright. Draw the peacock with its feathers down behind its back.

Step 3

Step 4

Final

Capuchin monkey

This small, furry monkey is cream or tan around the face, neck and shoulders. The rest of its body is dark brown. It has a white or pink face and a long tail that can wrap around tree branches. Long arms and human-like hands help this creature to move around its treetop home.

Capuchin monkeys dig for ants with sticks and use rocks to break open nuts. Draw a capuchin using one of these tools.

Step 3

Step 4

Step 5

continued on next page

Step 6

Step 7

Snow leopard

This rare cat has a body that is well-equipped for life in the mountains of Asia. The snow leopard is covered in a thick white, grey or yellow coat. Its fur is adorned with black markings called rosettes. Even its feet are covered with fur to protect its paws from the cold. Its muscular legs and tail provide the strength and balance needed to climb steep mountain slopes.

TIP

The snow leopard is a master jumper, covering six times its body length in one leap. Draw a snow leopard leaping through the air.

Step 3

Step 4

continued on next page

Step 5

Step 6

Step 7

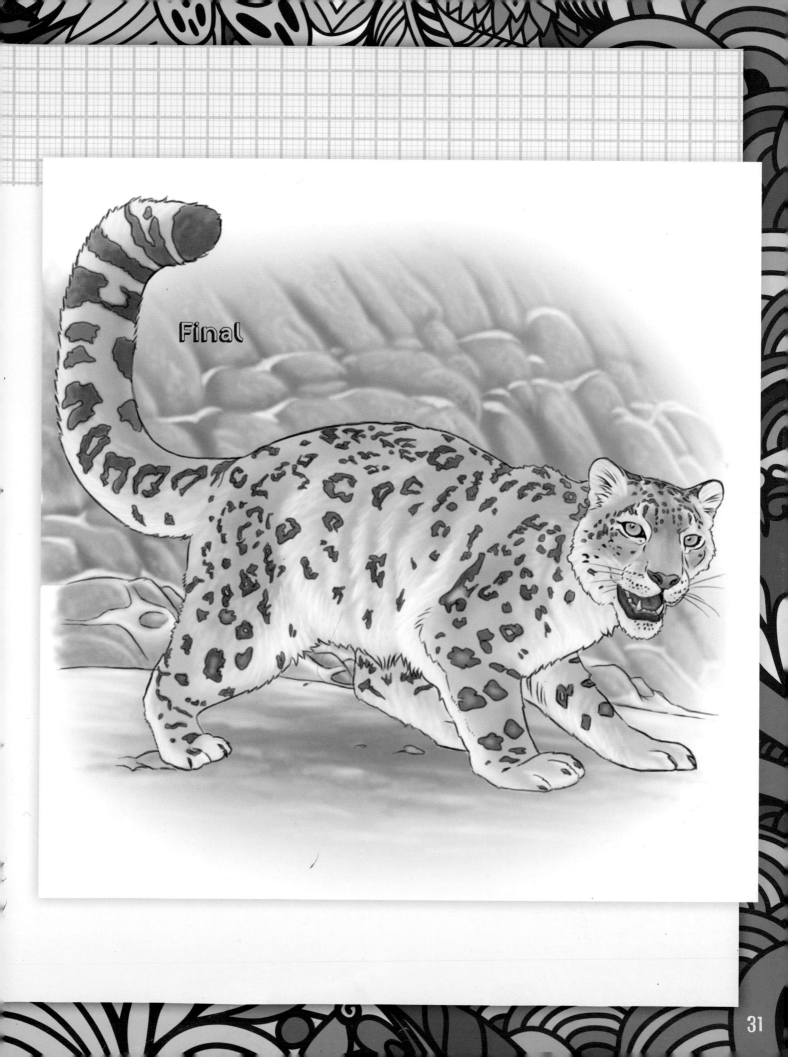

Final

Websites

www.bbc.co.uk/education/topics/zwc4jxs
Get creative! From pencils and inks to digital design tools, find hints and tips, including video demonstrations, for using all types of media and materials for your artwork.

www.bbc.co.uk/nature/animals/
Get inspired! Find hundreds of beautiful photographs and videos of the world's most amazing wild animals and try your hand at drawing them!

www.theguardian.com/childrens-books-site/series/how-to-draw
Learn from the experts! Follow these step-by-step guides and learn how to draw some of your favourite characters.

Look for all the books in this series!